TODAY CREATES TOMORROW

TODAY *Creates* TOMORROW

how DESTINY *lies in* YOUR *own* hands

stacey BLAKE

LW
LIGHTWALK PUBLISHING

*Scan this QR Code
to learn more about
this title.*

Publisher: Lightwalk Publishing, LLC.

paperback   ISBN-13 978-1-942692-06-5 | ISBN-10 1-942692-06-4
ebook   ISBN-13 978-1-942692-07-2 | ISBN-10 1-942692-07-2

Printed in the U.S.A.

1 3 5 7 9 10 8 6 4 2

For my loving husband

Tom

Table of Contents

Acknowledgments

ORD — THANK YOU FOR YOUR BLESSINGS AND GIFTS OF healing bestowed upon my mind, body, and spirit. May your loving hand continue to guide me in the work that I now do.

I live daily with sweetness inside my soul I never thought would be possible while here on this earth. My husband Tom and my incredible step-children Christina and Jeffery continue to be my anchor in this lifetime and I love them unconditionally.

I wish to thank each of my brothers for their devotion and love, Timothy most especially for his gift of life to me, his beautiful wife Debbie for believing in me and all that I am attempting to do now as an inspirational writer. To Jessica, Ryan, Martha, Brian, Marie, Ashley, David, Michael, and Billy - I love and bless you each. Mom, thank you for instilling within me the courage and belief that I could achieve all my dreams in life.

I offer here deep gratitude to my step-children's mother Susie – who has become a special friend to me. We share a beautiful energy that transcends the pains of this world. We have between us a deep "knowing" that we are joined via...*a divine mystical connection*. Angels have sprinkled sparkling golden light upon us gifting...*loving healing*...to all members of our extended families. Calmness, peacefulness, knowing of HIS ways, intersects all, offering strength, purpose, understanding, and rebirth.

Along the journey of our lives we sometimes cross paths with others whose entry into our lives we do not always understand the meaning of at first. Special friendships can arrive unexpectedly, especially when there is a *soul kinship*. **Spiritual** friendships often cannot be measured in the "quantity" of time spent together, but they usually arrive right on *schedule* and bestow light and love – *God's blessings.* Such is the case with two beautiful women I know: Connie Swaebe and Sue DeLoach. I met Connie several times over the past 10 years at my incredibly talented sister-in-law's home. I was always fascinated with her energy and the way she interacted with Susan. Something about Connie was just...*special.*

Writing *Today creates Tomorrow* took time for me to complete. I struggled as to how best to lay out the book's content. At a critical juncture in the book's birth, I reached out to Connie and her sister Sue for guidance. Both love and trust our Creator God, and each has walked the journey of their lives with some personal pain and struggle. When I called Connie for help, she and Sue immediately visited with me, offering prayers of confidence, grace, and trust. With their quiet beauty and tender touch, I was able to sort through the challenges I was experiencing. Thank you, Angels, for guiding these beautiful women to me!

Thank you Connie and Sue from the bottom of my heart.

I wish to extend a warm and special thank-you to two people with whom I share parts of my daily life and routine. My good friend and neighbor Sharon Smith and her husband Tom are not only wonderful friends but are dedicated to my personal comfort, feelings of security, and peace. Sharon and I share a special bond and mutual appreciation for the delicious things in life that are all around: our glorious lake and its beautiful sparkles and light reflection we are so fortunate to see each and every day. Like me, Sharon loves bird song, owl calls, the winds and sounds of nature, our animal friends, beautiful flowers, the twinkling of the stars, silvery moonlight, good wine, wonderful laughter, and the knowledge that all such gifts...*come to us from above.*

My best friend Kathy, whom I love without equal, is my true sister in spirit. She is courageous, beautiful, honest and loyal beyond my words here to convey. Kathy's place in my life is magical. Whenever I visit with Kathy, no matter how long it has been...*it is as if time has not passed but for more than a minute.*

To my readers – thank you for allowing me into your life. *May you be gifted with heavenly peace, strength, and the white light of love...*

Want to Change the World?

*Do one act of kindness each day of
the year and change 365 lives*

Anthony Douglas Williams

A Simple Prayer

N MY MEMOIR, *A SOFT LANDING,* I TALKED QUITE A BIT about the power of prayer – The Lord's Prayer especially – and why this prayer is so mystically powerful. But if prayer in this way has just never felt right for you, then I offer this simple, but very effective technique, for you to discover within yourself a connection to the ALL that is.

Place both of your hands over your heart
and say these words:

"I have all that I need within"
"I have all that I need within"
"I have all that I need within"
"I have all that I need within"

Repeat these words to yourself softly, slowly,
over and over and over.

Look deep inside your Heart while saying these words.

Say the words as long as you can until you begin to feel a slight vibration or maybe even a delicious feeling of "something" you may not have ever felt before.

That feeling is your soul in JOY.
It is the beginning of what true spiritual understanding and connection to ALL that is – feels like.
And the greatest secret of all is it lives right inside you every moment of every day.
The happiness you will feel inside your body is your soul jumping for joy saying – *I have been found!*
And that is the beginning of *everything!!*
Please try my simple prayer before reading this book. It may prove to be quite helpful.
Know though that if while reading, you encounter feelings of blockages or maybe even a slight headache, it could mean for you at this time, this one part of the book may not be timely.
No matter, simply skip this chapter or section and come back to it again at a later date, even if it takes a little while. Sometimes spiritual reading can feel "dense" and may be hard to absorb. That just indicates new pathways to higher knowing are trying to open and as with any new subject, be patient. Each rereading will bring bright new clarity.
There is no one direct "autobahn" route to deep spiritual learning and understanding.

But when you begin to accept and understand divine spiritual truths, your entire being and your life will shift slowly into tremendous happiness.

Farewell...My Beloved

THE DATE IS JUNE 11, 2014. I AWOKE THIS MORNING from an unexpected vision-dream. It had been a long time since my last one, and I had begun to think that maybe I would not have another while here on this earth.

I dreamt that I was at the original building lot of my food manufacturing company, which I wrote about in my first book, *A Soft Landing*. The company had closed its doors the year prior, in May 2013, and in one more week, all of our business assets will finally be sold.

The dream was vivid and very clear. I arrived at the site of my lot and it was completely empty except for this one part, where I could see several of my long-standing employees working hard to pull (up and out) from underneath the ground...what appeared to be a huge rectangular long block. It seemed cemented to the ground. Lots of hard digging was going on, and there were heavy stones lying all around. I could see they all were exerting hard effort, in trying to get this huge box unhinged from its spot. Curious, I walked over and asked what was going on.

"What are you guys doing here?"

"We cannot move this," one of them replied.

They appeared exhausted.

I took hold then the rope they were using, and with very little effort tugged at what looked to be the end side of a huge box. Immediately, out from under the ground…arose a huge beautiful chestnut-colored horse! With his saddle on, he shook himself deliberately, and he appeared a bit unsteady, as if he had been asleep for a while. I intuitively recognized him and felt within my heart this deep love and compassion for him. Automatically I bent my head down onto his and nuzzled his nose, hugging him hard, kissing deeply his forehead. Without any thought I began a prayer of gratitude and thanks to him. He responded by looking deeply into my eyes.

It hit me as a deep truth that we "knew" each other. Familiarity existed between us and I could sense it was very strong.

I had never met this horse before in a dream, nor was he a living horse belonging to anyone that I was aware of. Yet, I knew this horse, and he me, and suddenly I sensed that this moment we were sharing together was a heavenly gift. It was somehow clear to me…that this horse and I, that our time together, was now at an end.

This vivid dream I was having was to be our final *good-bye.*

Instinctively, I turned and led this beautiful horse away from the empty dusty lot. The lot instantly disappeared. As I walked the horse a bit further, I saw that he held himself with such amazing strength and poise; and as we walked, we stood before a large wide open field. It was meant for him. Seeing the beautiful space made me turn and look at my horse; I felt so happy for him...so very, very happy!

I awoke then, my heart feeling the lightest it had felt in years!

Sitting back on my favorite morning couch, I slowly sipped my iced coffee – realizing that this dream was another angelic gift. This vivid dream was a sign that my past, my incredible company, which I had built from scratch, some 30 years earlier, and which was so much a part of my soul...***is no more***.

"IT" was gone. "IT" and all that I had been before as a result of my long hard work finally was truly gone and over. And now like this horse – ***I am totally free.***

I feel exhilarated!!!

And yet...there is a strong sense of loss inside me. I am feeling the loss of my *spirit friend* (this horse) *I never even consciously knew existed.* But I know now that he did exist. And HE – as this *spirit-horse* – had been with me for over 30 years...through every single trial... **ALL** of my sufferings...my accomplishments...***my wins and losses; "HE" had always been with me.***

And now...he is destined to enjoy his freedom from all that hard work.

You may now be asking, What/who was this horse?

It took me several days to remember, but in 1986, when my company first moved into this building, I was at the time studying Native American Indian lore. I was participating in sweat lodges and fire walks, and was meeting several authentic medicine men and women from different tribes. One medicine man that I became friends with had come to my building one day, in order to perform a blessing for me. He walked the entire out-side building area "smudging" with sage (as it is called), cleansing, blessing and praying for my good fortune, protection, and guidance from the Great Spirit above, speaking words of courage for the trials and lessons ahead. In thinking about this day I recall how honored I felt watching him. I remember that I felt a tingling rush on my arms when I said good-bye to him, and how his eyes twinkled in a way that seemed to suggest he had left behind for me a secret gift somehow.

I know now what he gifted me with!

Horse Spirit – was **my medicine gift**. A form of "angelic presence" blessed upon me by my friend. Native American Indian wisdom teaches about animal spirits as being "medicine" from the Great Spirit, or God. In his form, as horse, this *spirit-being* existed deep within all that my company was, all that it stood for, and all that it was meant to be.

Horse medicine "gifts" a soul with *steadfastness, strength, integrity, "horsepower," capable of carrying heavy burdens for long miles…*this is what Horse universally is known for. And such was the truth of who and what I had been as my company's founder and its leader.

The Horse was me and I was the Horse, his spirit residing alongside my soul being. We were partners.

Horses throughout history have been loyal companions to humans in times of war, major battles, worldly exploration, farming, and industrialization. They have liberated man from the toils of work he could not have done without horses' assistance. The miracle of *knowing* now that I had this spirit animal, as my *medicine,* and that he had been with me through all my working years, moves me at the very center of my soul.

If someone had asked of me, "what spirit animal would you have thought was yours while you were working in the business-world," I would have answered, the lion, bear, or maybe the wolf. But in reviewing my incredible career, it makes such perfect sense that my animal spirit was Horse.

I know finally where my incredible dedicated love of horses comes from.

I never knew from where my deep love for horses of all kinds came, as I never rode horses when I was younger. But I LOVE horses and I want often just to be near them. I cannot watch any movie that depicts insult or injury to horses. Not Civil War stories or the like. Always I suffer a deep pain inside my soul that I just cannot explain. Whenever I see them raced, used in battles, or ridden too hard, I can become emotionally upset.

Now, I understand why.

And what is so bittersweet for me, in this realization, is that in so many small but deeply special ways,

I have always honored "Horse." In the small innocent actions that I just never really examined or thought about, such as my personal Facebook page, which is picture of a mother horse nuzzling her young foal so lovingly. And the fact that for many years I cannot drive by a horse farm without stopping and admiring all the horses, watching them enjoy their freedom, looking so happy and healthy. As well, I always imagine myself riding on top of a horse, feeling free and on top of the world. So it is without a doubt a blessing that I know what it is my inner soul wanted for me to finally "see" and to "feel": the "why" of my special connection to Horse. The intuition of this mystical truth that always, always, through all my years, "He" stood by me…strong, resilient, loyal, and brave…fills me full with deep, rich emotions.

Farewell, my beloved friend. May your days be light-filled and may you know how much I deeply love you.

Prologue

I COULD HEAR THE RAIN HITTING HARD THE LARGE-PANE glass windows in my living room. The weather outside had been cold and rainy for several days. I began to reread two emails sent privately to me by supermarket buyers, whom I had worked with for many years, asking me "where in the world were their orders." It was March 2013, and I had also just received, a week earlier, news from my oncology doctor that my leukemia (although very slight in its levels) had returned. I had begun new chemo medication, and I was once again feeling very tired.

I replied back to each buyer that I would attempt to find out immediately what was going on. I called the office and spoke with our customer service person, who answered me quite annoyingly that "she had not received any of these orders at all." Her tone was one of indignation and it was quite obvious to me that she felt totally inconvenienced by my phone call. Despite the fact that I had co-founded the company she worked for and had been its CEO for over 27 years, she was making it quite clear that my call, on this matter, was simply a bother. I could sense my body's rejection of her attitude and I began to feel quite angry.

I was able to ascertain quickly that, in fact, these orders had been received by the office, and for whatever reason, this young woman had not processed them properly. She had either chosen to ignore them, or she simply never checked the order inbox, which was the very first thing she was to do each morning. And now these orders, four in total, were late by almost two weeks.

I sighed deeply and lay my head down onto the desk. My company, which had been so finely run, for so many years (like a Swiss watch): every aspect – orders perfectly timed for their production, shipment, and delivery, all particulars carefully monitored and followed up on every day. Never did we miss the handling of order receipts, their shipment, supplies in, finished product out, or the prompt reply to any and all questions from our buyers and our customers. In those initial moments of realizing what was now happening, I felt like I had landed on an alien planet and that I was watching *someone else's company* coming apart at the seams.

But no, this was my company…and it was no longer functioning as well as it had for so many years. I realized in that moment, that like me, my company now had cancer.

My company was sick and it was getting sicker.
Some employees were displaying utter indifference,

such as I had never before seen. There was obvious discontent and after examining things a bit further, I could clearly see that the problem was not only front of the house (sales/admin), but back of the house too. I could sense a combination of emotions amongst certain employees I had spoken with. While many still sounded very loyal and committed, there was *(I could detect)* a distance in some of their voices, and I sensed there was a type of disconnect (a break in the rhythm) in what had always been such a viable and tangible "thing."

My company had stood for all that I had **loved** it into being. We had character, high-quality products, management integrity, purpose, excellent R&D, and smoothness of all operations and processes. And for so many years, it was a place of tremendous happiness, fulfillment, and unity. But now, in this moment, it was a shadow of its past. My employees, who had once been so dedicated, so enriched by all that we had together, had clearly lost their footing...and many on the inside were very angry. Angry, in truth, at me!

Mommy was never coming back...not ever!

What heartache.

In April of 2012, almost one year earlier, I had resigned as CEO/President.

The company's board of directors, aware of my circumstances, had not yet attempted to replace me. I had been by now on medical leave since December 2009, and while I did work on a very limited and part-time basis – overseeing and negotiating the most imperative circumstances for the company, troubleshooting, creating new brand names, approving new products, and contributing marketing guidance – I truly was an absent CEO.

And it is a fact that no company can last for long without a strong leader in that position.

Maybe a company if very well run can hang in for eight to twelve months, but I had by now been on medical leave for over three years. And no one inside the company had taken action, action that could have put into place a strong, healthy CEO. Why did they not hire someone of comparable talent, who could have taken over what had been for so many years an exceptionally well-run company?

Why did my partners and fellow shareholders not act?

Did they believe somehow that in my becoming so ill with cancer – I had abandoned them?

Today creates Tomorrow – how
destiny lies in your own hand.

CHAPTER ONE

The Courage to End That Which No Longer Should Be

S I REFLECT IN MY MIND ON THE PHONE CALLS THAT I had made during that terrible day, it was finally painfully clear to me that my company was no longer what it had once been. The tone of my customer service representative was icy, her whole demeanor defensive, and it was obvious now: she was just the tip of the iceberg. Many at this point no longer believed or felt the same about the company as they once had. And I intuitively sensed then, in that moment, that for some of my longstanding employees parts of them had died. They had in so many ways become lost. Without me there as I had been, what was needed next, for right redirection, was not going to magically appear out of thin air. While there were still many good, loyal employees, a few now had become bad eggs, and it takes just a few bad eggs to spoil **everything.**

After reviewing in my mind the depth of the indifference and blasé attitudes I had heard, it was indisputable that my company in the past year had turned a corner, and it was not ever going to come back around and become righted again without me.

The fact was I could never come back.

A decision happened within me. It came upon me with crisp clarity and deep certainty.

The time had come for me to shut my company down.

It did not matter to me that the company still had a strong grip on many intensely loyal customers, and that several of our products were solid winners. Creative new products had recently been developed and there was in front of us the real possibility of selling these new items on QVC, as well in more club stores nationally.

No, right now, in this moment, I knew that none of these facts mattered at all. It was crystallizing in my mind slowly that nothing the company attempted to do now or in the future would succeed, no matter what, as the essential glue that had built the company and had made it strong was gone. And that included more than just me. It was as if the foundation had cracked and water was slipping inside.

And while it was true that I was gone and I would never be able to come back, it was obvious to me (suddenly) that no one inside the company **GOT THAT TRUTH**. For a long time (over four years in fact) they had waited and waited for things to go back exactly the way they once were. And that reality could not be. I felt complimented by this as a possible truth, yet in many ways I was confused as well. I realized I too had been blind for a long, long time. And in this moment I felt as though I had just awakened from a long, hazy, disjointed sleep.

It took several weeks for me to coordinate my thoughts and to get the next steps right. I spent hours in silent prayer and deep quiet reflection. I knew deep in my heart that GOD quietly was signaling to me that it was time for me to move onto a new path, a new future. And in order to allow that new life's direction, I was facing in this moment what was going to prove to be the hardest, but most courageous action I have ever done in my life.

I was the one who must mandate that the company close down.

I realized deep in my heart that facing and surviving cancer had not been my most courageous personal act. No...the truth was that my leukemia would prove to have been a bit easier for me to conquer and deal with than what I needed to do now.

After long hours of thought and acceptance, I nodded my head at this knowing. It felt to me like I was facing a long jump off a cliff. I was afraid of the unknowns for everyone inside my company. What would happen to them, where would they go? Yet...I could feel throughout my body the comfort and the peace of God's loving hand upon me. "TRUST, Stacey"..."trust and surrender" had been his promise.

And so, with the angels by my side and love of my family safe in my heart, I did the bravest thing I had ever done in my life. In May 2013, I shut my company's doors for the very last time.

CHAPTER TWO

You Are Never Alone

A s I prepared to write this, my second inspirational book, I know that my deepest desire is to help readers connect to the power and love that lives right inside each and every person's heart. And when you make that connection, your life can truly change forever.

As we walk on this path of life, oftentimes we feel *that we are very much alone.* I have discovered for myself through so many years of suffering, prayer, and recovery that nothing could be further from the truth. Through long years of trials and tests, I found my way to prayer and from there, I learned that we (ALL) are surrounded by the white light of God. And, for each of us, there are guardian angels. They are with us every single minute of our lives. Never, ever, are we alone.

And while my first book is for the most part a memoir on how my spiritual faith helped me to survive my cancer, its message is more about **spiritual discovery**.

Each of us has the ability within our souls to communicate directly with our angels and to receive back confirmation that such communication is possible – via "signs." What many religions describe as the Holy Spirit is in fact a type of two-way communication intrinsic within each of us from birth. Activation of this direct connection with the angelic realm is similar to receiving and making a telephone call. It occurs without fail during earnest prayer and during times of intense crises. This "connection" to the angelic realm is a gift from our Heavenly Father and it remains "ON" every moment of your life. It is your choice whether you place a call with heartfelt belief, answer a call when heard, or ignore it altogether.

In my first book, I describe that for many years I would find feathers almost everywhere: on the ground right next to my car door, lying on top of my front steps at home, in front of my office door, on the street in front of where I was walking, etc. I did not know the meaning of it, but it seemed I was seeing feathers all the time. A few weeks after my near-death experience, I walked out of my home and was greeted with dozens and dozens of feathers! As I was standing looking at them spread out all over my front lawn, I began to feel an inner spinning (similar to vertigo) and within a few seconds "IT" clicked. Instantly I knew that these feathers were (and had been for years) a heavenly sign…a sign from my angels that I had never been alone and *I would never be alone – ever.*

My life changed!

This one part of my spiritual journey impacts readers so deeply that I receive note cards containing gifts of feathers and heartfelt stories of how feathers suddenly have begun to "appear" too many. I have been sent pictures of feathers being found lying next to my book. Others tell me that they have always seen (here and there) feathers during their lives, especially when they were sad, but it was not until they read my book that they began to *maybe understand why.*

It is so incredibly fulfilling for me to read these accounts as it is a validation and confirmation that in sharing my personal story, I have helped others to know (truly) that they themselves…***are never alone.***

It is always within your power to ask for help and guidance.

When you are ready for a sign (any sign) of comfort and assurance from above…simply ask. It may arrive as a song, a penny, the smell of a loved one's cologne (who may have passed), your grandmother's cooking or maybe even a feather! One friend of mine who so wanted to see feathers (and wasn't seeing them)…was driving behind a truck on the highway one day when suddenly the truck slammed on its brakes. Immediately dozens of chicken **feathers** flew out the back of the truck's bed onto her car.

Now that's an answer!

"You want to see feathers…well here you go."

"Ask and you shall receive."

Ask with sincere intention and you will not be denied. At the right *time* a sign will arrive.

**We are powerful energy beings
inside our physical bodies.**

It is a Divine Truth that we have within ourselves, *an enduring and abiding **light** to guide us,* which is there to surround our bodies with love and protection.

**It is our dismissal of this fact that is the
root cause of much pain and suffering.**

After having been through such difficulty during my earlier life, it was only when I finally made a solid connection to Divine Love that I was healed to the core of my being.

I found my way afterwards to experiences which validated, nourished, and nurtured within me tremendous strength, inner trust, and deep "knowing" that there truly is a Creator God who loves us. I was capable then of reaching in this lifetime heights of joy I had never thought possible.

I grew and came to learn what Divine Love really means and the gifts that knowing delivers.

And not one bit of it had anything to do with a specific religion, church, or organization of any kind.

I have come to learn that it is a type of (divine)

misdirection to allow "others" (spiritual gurus or ego-centric personalities) to hold your "soul's" maturity in their hands whereby you surrender your emotional and spiritual comfort to them and their leadings.

Your higher self...in hand with God...will guide you. When you make an inner commitment to yourself to allow your own higher self and angels to guide you Home...you will be led to the right books, the right prayers, and the right answers – for you.

For that magic to happen look within – inside your own heart and soul.

Waiting there is Divine Love!

Divine Love is what is most sacred in this world.

I hope that in sharing the amazing truths about how it is that your destiny as a soul (in all moments) lies in your own hands; as well, maybe if I can help you to understand the "whys" of life's seemingly unfair disappointments – such as my unexpected leukemia diagnosis, which led eventually to the closure of my business – that you can begin to distance yourself from anxiety, fear, and destructive emotions.

Holding close these Divine Truths, I am able to live every day free from anger, resentment, or frustration at myself, my partners, God, everyone.

I know that my highest good is safe, secure, and I am whole.

There are many ways to discover that God's love for each of us is real. It is in truth the only thing that I have found is absolutely **certain** in this life. But, how we connect with God and allow his love inside ourselves and our lives is an individual choice.

Just like any adventure, or in any climb up the mountain, you can take as long as you like, deviate off the path, enjoy long naps by the side of the trail, but a steady climb is always still in front of you. If you want to grow and accomplish greatness as a soul, having the Almighty as a part of your life makes the climb much easier! And you do not need to be an evangelist, a church member, or be committed to any one religion to have God as a partner in your life.

During my 30s and early 40s, I used to enjoy reading a variety of spiritual books. And while I was committed to reading these wonderful enriching works, I would oftentimes just devour a book's message, put it down, forget afterwards what I read, and continue to live in agony. That is, until "IT" finally clicked: the absolute knowing that God, as a source of deep love, really does exist. When that happened, it was like a clear spring of pure clean water running over me. I finally understood what living in true belief really meant and what followed were the gifts this *knowing* brought into my life.

Although there are many paths to learning that which is sacred, they all eventually lead to the one supreme truth. The Almighty, our Creator/God, this Universal Energy Source, loves us completely, and he **created** us...*so that we may love him in return.*

Walking in faith, knowing that God is good and that he is everywhere and inside every living thing provides important nourishment for the soul especially when times are difficult and the tests of life are all around.

After years of searching for spiritual truths I can say with total confidence that freedom from pain and confusion *rests in one's own hand.* It is not just the reading of inspirational works that will guide you Home at last.

It is in living these truths every single day. Therein lies the true magic.

> ***Every soul is on a journey in this life and the trials that come to us are a part of that journey.***

Make no mistake, just as young students in any school must be tested to confirm their understanding and depth of knowledge, so too does the Universe/God test us while here on earth.

"You claim you are devoted and loving" – **well,** be prepared to be tested by the Universe in some way to **"see"** if that is true.

"You claim you are generous, kind-hearted, and understanding" – be prepared to have several small seemingly insignificant opportunities arrive out of nowhere…to **"test"** that belief.

"You claim you are courageous and faith-filled" – be prepared to have a conundrum or paradox arrive in your life where your world will be turned upside down…to see if your faith holds you steady and true.

I have learned that we are tested while here on earth, we face "initiations" as they can be called, and we face trials and suffering – all designed and meant for our highest good and soul growth.

If your goal in life is to grow as a soul and to transcend the difficulties that may be all around you, it is really important to embrace within yourself an awareness that remains "present" or with you at all times.

This "awareness" will keep you alert to those small and seemingly insignificant tests that always come.

You can fail a test in innocent ways.

Maybe you pass that injured animal on the side of the road without even a blink or a second look to see if you could stop or call for help. **Or**, *you deny a friend a much needed hand with chores.* **Or**, *maybe you deny the offer of a small loan to a family member in real need.* **Or**, *maybe you deny someone his or her inner "peace" when they are desperately asking for your forgiveness on something you are still angry about.*

You have your good reasons, you have convinced yourself. You built your life the hard way, climbed your own ladder, and no one helped you – right?

Distance yourself from these invitations to be a kind soul, a loving friend, compassionate and forgiving, and watch how YOUR life can become a bit tangled, confusing, and stuck. **That promotion you wanted so badly...*passes to someone else*. You are driving on a long trip or vacation...*and you find that delays, inconveniences beset you everywhere*. You search for that perfect new house...*which you cannot locate, and when you do – someone else buys it before you do*.**

Frustration, anger, and even fury can become now your new reality when only months ago…

You thought you were like Buddha.

"Initiations" or life's tests are necessary, and they happen to everyone in one lifetime or another, in order that the soul may grow and reach its highest potential in "god-consciousness" and light. Easy carefree lives, while not a bad thing necessarily, may not always offer the best chance for soul growth. It is oftentimes only through adversity and difficult trials (sometimes excruciating in their impact) that a soul develops and grows.

How you handle and resolve these challenges as they arise determines entirely how your life will unfold.

Today creates tomorrow.

There is no escape; and there are no short-cuts. Your destiny lies in your own hands.

Life is Eternal

N MY FIRST BOOK I DISCUSS MY NEAR-DEATH EXPERIENCE, which changed me in a way I did not fully understand at the time. It was not until a few weeks later that I experienced an epiphany. In one split second it was as if everything I had ever read, felt I understood spiritually, and had experienced ''sunk'' deep inside my soul and into every cell of my body. All my angelic experiences, mystical and inspirational books that I had read, all my meditations, prayers (seeing feathers), and even meeting my angel at the door to the afterlife collided together inside me in a way that hit me like a bolt of lightning.

Instantly I knew what it was to fully believe and know God in every fiber of my being.

This knowing changed me forever.

It was impossible for me thereafter to keep believing that I was still a "seeker."

I was not.

I had become whole inside and I have never been the same since.

It was May 2001 and I had been in many ways "reborn." Not reborn facilitated by any specific religion, or church group, but "reborn" inside myself where my inner soul resides.

I feel that my years following that one particular day in May 2001 were a final preparation for me to enter what is now the most *glorious time of my life*. I am free from all of the hard work I had been consumed with for years. My husband and I live free from my disease and the setbacks that caused, and we are reorienting our lives towards what we know will be our happiest years together.

So while it is very true that I did *suffer* during many years of my life and I did experience deep physical, mental, and emotional pain...that chapter for me is at an end.

This truth does not by any means ensure that while I remain here on earth, I will not have further challenges or disappointments.

I simply handle them much differently than I ever did before.

Spiritual journeys can be enthralling.

Along the way you may travel to exotic lands, experience exciting varied cultures, partake in unique beliefs, study other religions, and you can immerse yourself in many wonderful spiritual books, lectures, and meditations providing delicious experiences beyond your wildest dreams.

However, while all of that is enriching and intellectually insightful, it may remain in many respects a shadow-like existence, until and only until, that **"click"** happens inside your soul.

What you really want and what evaded me for years is that internal **switch** that will permanently turn ON, and when turned on, it will ***reorient your every thought, word and deed...forever.***

When this happens, your search for divine understanding will bloom in a significant way and you will find yourself easily satisfied in the very basic TRUTHS about our Creator.

You will in time begin to take great pleasure with just the simple things in life. *A kindness extended by a stranger, a smile, a warm loving hug, the comfort of a pet, the smiles and screams of joy from little children, bells ringing, birds singing, and just the intoxicating smell of fresh air.*

Being alive and awake in this way is the greatest gift you can ever experience.

Finally, and most importantly you will be at rest in the search for that *"next bit of esoteric knowledge."*

An insatiable hunger can sometimes come round

from having read many of the great mystical books ever written, which are incredible to read and to experience, but which will only take you so far.

A "seeker" is not a "master."

You will obtain **mastership ONLY** when you have secured inside your soul the deepest peace you will ever know. **"Knowing"** what your relationship to God/our Creator really IS, you will achieve a rich profound "quietness" to your mind.

You live then with full awareness of the energy essence of God and the Goodness that does gift.

You will understand finally that you **"serve"** by being whole and complete at last.

> *My life's purpose today is no longer about addressing the demands of a hungry growing company and the long hours of hard work to keep a company afloat in today's economy.*

I have come to understand that souls **"serve"** the Universe best by walking gently on their road, carrying out their remaining earthly duties and responsibilities with less anxiety, stress, fear, and anger.

Peaceful souls bless the earth with every step they take, every smile they give, and every hand they shake.

**Just BEING peaceful...will spread in
small steps PEACE everywhere.**

Remaining peaceful is your highest obligation (once you achieve it) because when you are at peace you are one of God's "light workers." And while many seekers feel they are here only to complete some kind of hard work or to prove themselves in their ability to make money, provide a good home to their family, etc., it is when you transcend that limited mind-set that you become a living "master," a "light-worker," **and the greatest gift you offer, then, is you!**

Your reason for being here on earth will change, and your purpose will become clear. Spreading **"light"** in any way you feel motivated is all that is necessary. You can still be whatever you **are** in your life…a janitor, a secretary, a musician, a nurse, a business owner, a policeman, a bartender; any job works *as what you do for work is not the issue.*

> ***It is the love you spread as you are working that is the key.***

When you are **"awake"**…knowing you are a **"light-worker,"** you will in time desire less material things, need fewer expensive experiences, and your entire reason for waking each day will become transformed.

You also may no longer desire or feel the need to align your soul growth to any spiritual teacher or guru who claims a special knowledge of God.

And while I feel a deep inner calling to write about our Creator and His Divine Truths, I do not wish to do so in any manner that "binds" people to me. Seekers who are sincerely searching for personal spiritual freedom – I hope my words have an effect in helping them find their true path (their way INTO their own hearts)…where all God's divine truths live.

There are many **extraverted personalities** today in the various spiritual movements who are monetizing themselves by way of claiming every two to three years "new enlightened spiritual or scientific knowledge" of God's universe and the "whys" of our earthly existence, our soul history, parallel universes, quantum jumping, etc.

Much of what is written and spoken about by others is **intellectually** very interesting, and can provide you a great time of it with many people to talk to, blog sites to read, conferences to attend, and sacred places to visit here on earth.

However, I have found for myself that this method of spiritual discussion and activity did not align my soul in a place of long-lasting comfort and peace.

I discovered that too much activity (this way and that) can cause a disruption of sorts internally, whereby you are no longer engaged in a dedicated search "within." Instead your search is "outwards" – away from the divine inner soul's connection that lives always (within you)...and ***which is the only place on this earth where you will find calmness, centeredness, deep everlasting peace, and connection to The Almighty.***

You can experience from different spiritual activities a brief transitory "sense" of being connected, but it often is fleeting – leaving you feeling bereft of ("a something") you were truly longing for. Necessitating (possibly) that again and again you open your wallet and spend more money to go here, there, and everywhere in an effort to once again re-capture a small energy vibration hook-up that oftentimes circulates inside spiritual group activity.

I promise you…when you are near death and especially in the last few moments of your life you will not be seeking nourishment from outer sensory experiences. Knowledge of the physics of the Universe will not provide you with any inner warmth.

What you will crave and what you will want to KNOW for certain inside your heart

Is that you are unconditionally LOVED.

Your soul will long for quietness of spirit – secure in the knowing that you are

***Loved by ALL that IS – that you are
Safe – and that you are going Home.***

You will not care a whit about your riches, missing your earthly pleasures, your next intellectual feat, or any other such nonsense.

In the last few seconds of your life – it ALL comes down to the exact same thing for each of us:

**Unconditional Love, Forgiveness,
Grace, and a Peace-filled Soul.**

I hope to help you secure this connection to Divine Love that is available within you always.

**Because once you find IT – you
will never lose IT again.**

And no matter how many years you have left on this earth to live, you will begin to live free from an inner turmoil, that nagging anxiety and doubt about whether you are LOVED by our Creator and whether there was "purpose" to your life and your soul's journey.

When you connect to your higher self and you find within your heart The Almighty...you will KNOW for certain – all the rest of your days – who you are – who God is – and you will feel forever after that you are ***loved, safe, and totally secure in his protection and care.***

To begin the initial steps of this life-changing transformation inside yourself, it is helpful for you to become acquainted with what are often called *UNIVERSAL TRUTHS*, as they are a part of (as well as true for) every living entity here on this earth, in all worlds and universes...in every DNA cell – all living beings – everything!

I can assure you that **knowledge and acceptance of** these *DIVINE TRUTHS* will align intense comfort deep within you.

While these truths are part of the all the universes and all of which our Creator is – you may find in this lifetime one particular truth very stimulating to your soul's growth.

For me that Universal Truth is:

Life is Eternal. We are forever.

What does this mean?
Universal truths are a little bit like magic.
Before delving into them, please try to refrain from trying to "intellectualize" and tear apart any one of

these "truths" into small digestible pieces, so that there is a precise knowing for you in all things of this world.

It is not possible for any person to know **ALL** that there is to know about how the Universe and God works.

Our minds simply cannot comprehend it as we are in our bodies today.

Luckily we do not need to **know** all in order to grow and mature as a soul.

Releasing yourself from the destructive patterns of needing to rip every single thing apart is the best, most liberating act you can do to allow yourself to be FREE from the frustration and anxiety of having to UNDER-STAND it ALL.

It is not possible for any human being, no matter how brilliant, to understand the inner workings of the Universe, GOD, and his whole divine plan.

We may not have all the answers and we may never know everything...

But we can understand some of it!!

The best example that I can provide to help explain this plainly is that of the rose. You see a beautiful rose. YOU do not need to rip that rose apart, petal by petal, in order to try and ascertain the *"why"* of how it is a rose.

It simply is. It is a rose.

And you can enjoy this rose, as it is, without destroying it.

I love roses. I surround my home with roses in my garden and I love it when my husband brings home roses for me. They lift me up and make me so happy and their aroma is for me a type of healing. And so, I wish to offer this as an example…to help in the deeper understanding of how I understand divine universal truths.

They just are true!

Like the rose, you can smell it, enjoy its beauty, and it is therefore for you a gift.

Divine Laws are like the Rose.

Simply accept their truths and you will benefit!

I believe that this trait – *our human desire to question over and over the full meaning of God, and his ways – this fracturing of spiritual learning into small tiny boxes* – is why so many people give up their desire to understand the deeper meaning of life.

Please try to receive some of my words on universal truths and *accept* them…as they are without your mind causing an argument within…and a *"light"* inside your own heart…your "intuition"…may begin to vibrate and you will begin to *feel the truth*…and when you do a doorway to higher knowing will appear quite readily inside you.

Like the rose – Divine Laws
simply ARE true.

Tearing apart a rose causes permanent injury; **it no longer IS a rose**.

I have seen people do this to themselves. You can do this same type of injury to yourself in your desire to know the deeper truths about life, God, and happiness. Tearing apart, bit by bit, any one aspect will destroy within you the chance to admire and enjoy that which just IS true.

Thankfully, we cannot destroy any one Universal Truth's real essence.

While the rose torn apart may be gone and no longer alive...ROSES themselves are not destroyed.

**They will continue to bloom
wherever life chooses.**

Such is the case with every single one of the Divine Universal Truths.

Your attempts to tear one or more truths apart, bit by bit, may destroy **YOUR** ability to enjoy the benefits of such truths, **but the truth itself is never destroyed.**

How to best understand that which is not easily understood? Read slowly some of the words written; meditate deeply on some of the statements. Select other works or readings to help deepen your understanding. Reread as many times as you need to because when you finally feel that long sought-after connection, that "click" – a richness unlike anything you have ever felt before will awaken inside you, and thereafter, your search will become fuller and more complete.

Universal truths, once you accept them...flow...one into the next, and gradually you will begin to deeply understand LIFE and all of the mysteries that have befuddled many of us for so long.

It is a journey into joy.

Life is Eternal. It is forever and everlasting. My deepest hope is you will allow inside your own heart the knowledge and faith that there is no death at the end of this life.

The spirit goes on into other dimensions in the afterlife and continues its growth.

The veil that shields our eyes while we are here on earth is removed when you die from this life and pass onto the next.

And as with what happened to me during my near-death experience, when I was released (unzipped) from my body…for just a few minutes, you will understand (in an instant) what IT is, and what **IT** – your life – has really been all about.

I promise you that you do not need to die first to gain the benefits of what I hope to offer here.

Spiritual knowledge and release from much pain can happen for you very quickly…***but only if you allow it.***

Scientists have recently been able to understand the meaning of *dimensional reality* and that all life is connected via energy threads.

Picture the earth from afar as if you are in space. See the earth wrapped within a web of interconnecting lines (called threads or "strings") that go around and around and around over and over again crisscrossing each other. Physics is beginning to understand that such energy lines are dimensional and they contain within them realities such as what we are living here on earth. (For more understanding on this, please refer to Gregg Braden's book *Divine Matrix* in the Recommended Reading.

Scientists have discovered that all things material are in fact not solid. Your table, chairs, car, and everything you touch are not actually "solid." They are composed of energy which exists within Divine Law and appear, feel, and behave as if they were solid.

We as well are etheric beings: here on this earth to grow, but upon death, our soul (our true essence) is free and our *"god-conscious eyes"* will be open.

The dense matter which holds us as we are now here on earth will be gone when we are HOME again surrounded by light and love. Those of us who have been at the doorway to the afterlife, and have seen a glimpse into this truth, carry deep inside ourselves a *hum*, a vibrational recognition of this truth...*that there is no real death*. And what awaits us in the afterlife is a dimensional reality that looks and feels like earth. There are homes, mountains, lakes, and things familiar such as what is now our human everyday life – the only difference is that you will control your reality and experiences via your thoughts.

For me, I describe in great detail the near-death experience that I had. It gifted me with a taste of what it is to be free of this earth.

And that glimpse has changed my life forever.

Religions try to teach us that there is a heaven. That God has provided a home, safe and secure for us all.

But how does one know that for sure?

I believe this one question is always in the back of everyone's mind while they sit in Sunday school as children or as adults in church. I know that for myself, I always wondered about this *"place"* called heaven.

Does it really exist?

How does anybody really know?

Well, I know it does exist because I stood at heaven's doorway as my angel showed me inside my mind this truth. I *felt* heaven's presence as I was considering **"do I want to stay in this life or not?"** In those moments, I had been released from the bounds of my body and the feeling of peace inside me was indescribable. Glorious in every way one can imagine. And this feeling, this deliciousness, I can still tap into within me today when I need to *remember.*

And there are on earth today thousands more people like me who have had the courage to speak or write about their near-death experiences.

*We are here now on earth as "witnesses" to
the glories which await our return.*

Many of my spiritual readings have been from departed "soul beings" who offer love and comfort to us while we remain here on earth. White Eagle's teachings are one of my favorites because his messages always vibrate a high energy of Love. It can be felt in every word and on every page. And every time I read writings by White Eagle, I feel a resonance – a bit of that *"hum"* that I felt so strongly when facing the doorway to the afterlife.

CHAPTER FOUR

The Divine Plan

Divine Truths = Divine Law

OUR HEAVENLY FATHER'S DIVINE PLAN FOR OUR earth world, and all the Universes, is for his children, his "creations," to grow in the knowledge of their Divinity, to understand their connection unto **HIM**, **HE** unto us, (**all**) living beings, human, angelic, animal, energy light beings, etc., to go forth, experience adventures, fall down, get back up, and return **HOME** unto **HIM**.

And as with earthly laws, breaking Divine Laws does have consequences.

As with my own personal story I struggled for many years to understand "why" my life had been at times quite difficult, despite the fact I was a good person and was very much committed to professional ethics in my business's work and to generosity for my friends and family.

While rewarding and satisfying in many material ways, several of my adult years were in truth lonely and difficult. And when the deepest personal happiness I had ever known finally *arrived for me*, my life took a sudden and desperate turn.

I was diagnosed with leukemia.

I have previously shared a lot of information about the winding spiritual path that assisted me in surviving such a traumatic event as my cancer, and here in this work, I hope to impart that it is in the **acceptance** of divine truths which my or anyone's spiritual journey, in the end, *is really all about.*

It can take many years to develop true attunement for deep spiritual understanding.

As someone who spent many years searching for the answers to life's meaning, I can say with some confidence that it is helpful (really helpful) to simply **accept** that Divine Laws are not passive.

By that I mean...just saying prayers by rote or in a mechanical way, **without *deep feeling*,** and by going through the mechanical motions of religious rituals, ***without thought***, or attending spiritual conferences may not lead to deep lasting peace OR the release of painful suffering.

Just showing up to church or temple does not always hold the keys to unlocking life's riddles.

So where do the answers really lie?

Well, there are several places to search, but that activity alone may not satisfy. To really allow a release of pain you have to be active in your quest.

You must be **active** in how you, yourself, think, speak, interact, and dream.

You need to accept...really accept, Divine Truths as being TRUE...no matter who you are, where you live, or the color of your skin.

Universal laws as they sometimes are called, when adhered to, and deeply *accepted,* assist us on our journey through this life.

You can arrive at great spiritual knowledge through your intellect alone. That is true for many people. Use of your mind can lead to much information. You can even learn much about the magic of the universe, the physics of it all, of all the stars and solar systems, and just how perfect we are scientifically.

But,

UNTIL you open your **HEART** and begin to really *feel...the divine love of all that is...***THE DIVINE LOVE THAT LIVES NOW (*RIGHT NOW*)... INSIDE YOUR OWN HEART** and you demonstrate this knowing and love daily **in all your affairs...**

You will remain asleep.

The path to the deepest peace you will ever know is the path of

Love, gentleness, and self-discipline.

To live this truth in **"every thought...word and act"** is the secret pathway to **JOY** and perfect happiness.

*There are no short-cuts into
heavenly understanding.*

The path is narrow, difficult, and full of trials.

But, step by step, the soul learns to be strong, steady, and poised. The soul learns to withstand the storms that will always come.

**You cannot climb through any
window into heaven.**

You have to enter through the doorway.

I offer this sacred tip to you. Welcome your lessons, your difficulties, and your trials whether you believe you deserve them or not.

It is a promise from our Creator that if we live according to Divine Laws while here on earth we can experience deep serenity, self-control, and peace while we go along on our earthly journey.

This is the key *secret* to surpassing and overcoming ALL of life's hardest trials and suffering.

WELCOME every difficulty as it arrives, thanking it for its purpose in guiding you **HOME** to your place of deepest peace and happiness.

All trials in life come to you to *aid* in the strengthening of your soul so that you can touch your heavenly home while here on earth and gain entry into our heavenly afterlife prepared for us above.

Where we all wish to return and be forever.

My leukemia was a significant "test" for me in that for years I had been strengthening and developing my inner soul's resilience. What greater way for me to demonstrate my inner faith and trust in God than in facing my cancer unafraid and with the knowledge that I was safe?

**My illness was for my soul a
specific initiation for me.**

However, such tests are not always singular in nature and purpose.

They arrive as well to "test" those around us.

**How each of us handles and
"REACTS" to the testing determines
how one's life unfolds.**

Every decision and reaction today determines always our tomorrow.

It can be no other way.

These divine truths (of which there are many) are in reality the very essence of our universe, our earth world and beyond.

Science is now just beginning to really know and understand that these laws – especially in the world of physics – do exist. And in this **knowing**, scientists are confirming that which prophets and mystics have known for thousands of years.

There is wholeness, a connectedness: an etheric energy thread (perfect and true) to all of life.

Follow these truths and you will find your way **Home:** your true home of spirit, love, and peace.

The biggest lie that most people come to believe about life (after they have been beaten around a bit) is that the world **is random and chaotic.**

If you have wondered **"why"** your life has not been progressing the way you had always hoped, try to allow deep inside yourself the belief that these (unchangeable) divine universal laws once known and deeply accepted… **will absolutely help you to conquer suffering!**

Once you allow acceptance of these universal truths and laws inside your body and mind, there can be an immediate feeling of deep reassurance within you.

And your life, which may have felt out of control for many years, can finally come under control.

A transformation for you will occur.

Whatever your religion, the same precise universal laws apply. The highest of them is this:

God is pure love.

God is with you, inside you, guiding you, and holding you in his arms at all times, most especially through difficult and desperate episodes.

Such as my leukemia and my partner's inactions to save the incredible company I had built.

God is divine law and divine law is love!

When you understand this one truth, a knowing will come to you that allows you to "see" that cohesion (a glue) exists between **all things** in this world...and you will begin in steps to sense the strength of it...and you will feel finally – the truth – that Divine Laws are **binding** in all matters...and **this understanding**...will release you from fearing that you are **alone and powerless**.

YOU ARE NEVER ALONE

Acceptance of God *as Love* and that *Divine Law is Love*...is the foundation for all happiness.

This divine truth, this knowing deep inside me, helped provide me with clear insight into the "whys" of my own pains and struggles. It was time for me to be walking down a very different road. My past is no more. That which was true no longer is true for me.

In recognizing this truth, there can only be "good" in all things; even those things I/we believe may be undeserved or "bad."

They are not "bad"; they simply are happenings we did not want to see, but they happened anyway.

And in accepting them, in trusting that which we do not yet understand the reasons for, we find ourselves facing a deeper truth – the universal truth of where we belong and where we are heading next.

The Almighty's hand directly affected the inactions of my partners.

They could not help but do that which they were guided to do, which was to not act.

God had his plan for me and it no longer involved

my being strapped to or worried about a company I could no longer be a part of.

The same plan **HE** had as he guided the hands of my doctors, who saved my life.

And while I do understand intellectually these universal truths…

It was in LIVING through my experiences with faith and confidence that all would be well…that I confirmed for myself that I was "connected," "trusting," "whole," and "safe" through it all.

And while I suffered sadness and grieving for my company and all that we stood for,

**I am the HAPPIEST…I have
ever been in my life!**

All, each of us, when we allow divine love into our lives – we begin to respond to our higher selves… guided by the divine light which is our Creator's love whether we consciously, fully, realize it or not.

And if we believe that this truth is TRUE, then the most loving actions my business partners did for me were to follow their personal inclination to do nothing!

Because that is what **HE** wanted…
and they collectively obeyed.

And I love and respect them completely for this.

This "truth" that all life is energetically connected by love (from every person to each other)…all life…all humans…all animals…and all things…**IS** the answer to **everything**.

Acceptance of the Divine Laws of life assures your soul of success in its search for harmony and equilibrium.

ALL, each of us, **ALL** life is guided and governed by this highest universal law, and **THAT** law again is **LOVE**.

Climb the heights into heaven and **God** is there waiting for you.

Descend into the depths of hell, and God is there too.

God IS, HE is ALL and God is Love.

How extraordinary!

Why is this so important a fact to know?

Because when you understand this truth deeply, calmness abounds.

It will arrive into your life and release you from so much duress. When the mind and heart let go of the fear that *"the world is out to get you,"* that there are *"bogey men"* out there trying to *"defeat you"* and that life is *about failure, pain and desperation*, **true peace** can come into life, *your body, and your mind*.

And it can stay there forever.

As I learned for myself, after much pain and suffering,

God is ALL; He is in ALL things, HE is everything, He is everywhere, and He is pure love.

The yin/yang, the dark/light, day/night, goodness/evil, it all is God. Like a theatre play, God's purpose is for the growth of every soul's journey HOME.

That means YOU.

Once you really understand and accept this truth; *that nothing in life and no one can ever really hurt you...* because everything is God (and God is you) and that **HE is all around you**, then and only then, **FINALLY...** your world and your purpose for being here on earth will make sense.

My joy in writing this book is to help anyone who is truly ready to understand - **living "God consciously"** is possible.

Believe – that if you have found your way to my book, on many levels you are ready to be free of pain, confusion, and suffering.

Being truly aware of the cosmic universal laws that do exist means that as an "awakened" soul, you can utilize the gifts of The Almighty to live in harmony and peace at last.

Arriving at this place of peace may happen very quickly for you or it may take a few more years of trying, many more readings, and rereading, of the right books, and many more sleepless nights questioning the "why" and so on.

**Know though that despite that zig/
zag path – deep down you are ready.**

There are many wonderful other books that you

can also read to reinforce some of what my own words may ignite for you. (See Recommended Reading for some selections.)

CHAPTER FIVE

Time Has No Meaning

WORRY NOT IF YOU FEEL YOU HAVE WASTED many years during your life. The next most important Universal Truth about the Creator's plan for us as humans is that TIME...as we understand it here on earth...is *meaningless.*

Time is eternal, it is forgiving, and it is forever.

TIME MEANS NOTHING.

Divine Laws have been given to mankind since ancient times through Moses, Jesus, Mohammad, Buddha, etc. Since the beginning of creation, the truth about life and how to live life in peace and happiness has been told in parables, psalms, poems, and prayers, but mankind has been quite unable to hear.

We have rejected many of these truths, but these truths are unchangeable.

They exist whether we believe them or not.

God in his love for us has never abandoned or withdrawn from our world. It takes only a moment of full understanding of this truth to make a great change, and that change can be made inside you.

**Change yourself and change
for the world can begin.**

This is how destiny lies in your own hands.
We are not powerless, nor are we victims.
God's love holds a deep compassion for us **ALL**.

In truth, we are HIM and He is US.

It took me years to finally understand and release my attachment to the "theatre of life" that is always present. It is the **NOW** and we are in it *(playing our roles through good times and bad).*
What is the "theatre of life"?
The "theatre of life" is all the dramas that people cling to every day – greed for money, fear of poverty, committing acts of betrayal and fear of being betrayed, abandonment, jealousy, arrogance, glamour for celebrity, loving riches and those who are rich, envy, power, excessive eating, drinking, drugs, etc.
The "theatre of life" once you are entangled can lead you down a nowhere path into pure

nothingness – *resulting in intense loneliness, confusion, emotional pain, and feelings of worthlessness.*

ARRIVING finally to a place of true peace…is the struggle most of us deal with every day.

Learning and accepting any of the Divine Laws can mean at long last your pain, your struggles, and your body can finally be healed. It is a divine truth that you can have all of the incredible wonderful things our human life experience offers, but it is in *how you achieve them* and how you *handle it* when you have all that you always desired (in hand)…that will determine whether you are living awake in the light of God's love or **not**.

How you **achieve** your riches and your power OR how you handle your lack of riches and power, as well your daily treatment of all living creatures and peoples, will determine *everything for your soul* – in this life and the next.

Your reality, your life as you live it now, **is a result of an ongoing circular stream of energy generated by you.**

You can attempt in various ways through visitations to psychics, meditative alternate reality tricks, hypnosis, and even "dreaming" to uncover your soul's spiritual history and purpose; however, such information or experiences often can lead you unsuspectingly into intense, complex, and disturbing feelings.

You may become paralyzed in the belief that you have been for many lifetimes – *a victim*.

This is a trap!

I promise you – if you can **accept** as true that you are never a victim, not ever, and that you are a part of a family of souls on a long journey HOME – making mistakes along the way…

No matter whether you feel abandoned,
cheated, betrayed or unloved

Or whether YOU have abandoned,
cheated, betrayed or denied love

**You will "see" life and "experience"
life so differently.**

You will leap for joy when those mental and emotional burdens you no longer could tolerate are released by you and gone!

You will savor and enjoy (the why) of what once appeared (as hardships) you saw as so unfair…turned into gifts of opportunity that will aid **YOU**…in achieving your heart's deepest wish.

And your soul's deepest desire is to know that, despite everything you have been through,

You are loved.

**You are infinitely loved and protected
by our Creator always and forever.**

Allow this love and knowing into every cell in your body and watch your life become delightful.

My deepest desire for those reading here my words is to merge my inner voice, *my personal knowing,* with the *rich beautiful divine truths* I have come to accept over the years.

*It is up to you to allow such peace
to bloom inside yourself.*

CHAPTER SIX

The Spiritual Beauty of Suffering

WHETHER YOU ARE IN YOUR 30s, 50s, 70s, OR older, know that when this life ends for you, no matter how much you may have suffered, when die you, you will be free finally of all that disturbed you.

You will not be free however from the lessons such suffering was meant to teach you.

Suffering leads to soul growth.

There are thousands of examples of this to observe throughout history: Jesus most especially.

Suffering IS a necessary initiation along the path to soul growth.

The **secret** is your "**reaction**" to suffering, as it is occurring.

This is the next most important universal truth to digest and understand.

How you have "**reacted**" all during your life, to the trials, and the challenges that met you along the way, will determine how soon you return back to earth to try again.

And believe me; you will want to return and to try again.

Because when you are free of the bondage of your body – when you are free of the emotional storms which may have beset you all through your life – you will, upon entering heaven, ***understand*** that you could have done better (tried harder), been more *forgiving, loving, trusting, surrendering*, etc.,

And you will long very much for a renewed opportunity.

It is what the soul's evolution, our path, is all about.

And when you are free from your problems (and your human body) and after you become **refreshed**, you will want more than anything else to try again!

"Remembering"…**more divine truths while here on earth next time.**

And the most important thing for your soul to remember is that you are *loved deeply*; YOU are a child of the Almighty and your soul is *forever safe*.

There are many ways to find your way home to God, our Heavenly Creator, and one of them is to understand the life of Jesus.

Jesus was a human being (a man), but he also was **The Son of God** as the Holy Bible describes.

What in the world does that mean?

When you deeply accept divine truths, your "god-conscious eyes" will open and your heart and mind will finally be free from all that has confused you. You can then uncover within yourself an incredible sacred knowledge and truth about Jesus.

Like you, Jesus was born as a human being, but He was in His divinity fully "awake"; complete in "god-consciousness."

What is often referred to today as CHRIST CON-SCIOUSNESS...and being "Christ Conscious" means to live fully awake and aware that you are a child of God. It is a "state of being," a knowing, that our Creator is within you at all times *and at all times you are with HIM.*

Whether you are religious or not, Christian, Jewish, Buddhist, or Muslim – IT just IS TRUE.

Jesus – "The Christ" describes the man Jesus who was "The Christ" in his fully awakened faith-filled state.

*Awakening and being "Christ Conscious"
is available and within us all.*

That is one of the highest Divine Truths.

And it requires no religious affiliation to be *TRUE.*

We all can be "awakened" while here on earth. We all have the ability to experience miracles. And we all have the ability to heal our fellow man.

We all are striving whether we are aware of it or not to be awake and "god-conscious."

Jesus demonstrated many divine truths.

Yet, Jesus was a human being, a man, who was capable of the same anger, deep pain, and fear you have experienced.

While Jesus was **"GOD-CONSCIOUS"** and in so being was the true **Son of God,**

He was a man of flesh and blood.

If you can suspend for yourself some of the "words" traditionally used within religions and religious ceremony about Jesus, and allow this simple visual inside your mind and heart, you will gain much understanding.

Jesus is a wonderful example to think about when you wish to transcend the ignorance of the world, the dogma which sometimes reduces religions to a polarizing argument and which devalues what it is you really desire to finally understand as a soul.

There is no **one** religion in this world which is the only one to guide you to your heavenly home.

Each religion has truth, each holds community and fellowship, and each is special in its own way. And all human beings no matter their religion or no religion hold the same "seeds" within their soul to be fully "awake" and "god-conscious."

Jesus himself was a human being whose divine mission while on earth was to demonstrate that

**"The Kingdom of Heaven" lies
within one's own heart.**

*(Trust in the Wisdom of your Heart...
it will lead you HOME)*

And regardless of religion, when one looks deeply into the facts of Jesus' mission while here on earth, you cannot help but feel incredible *awe*.

But in honoring the memory of Jesus – it is important to remember that Jesus was deeply afraid the night before his crucifixion. He suffered a type of deep spiritual anguish and agony over what was to come for him, and he begged God in the Garden of Gethsemane to release him from what was to come.

Jesus lived fully aware that He as "The Son of God" was going to die a horrible death. And just as we are oftentimes afraid of facing the consequences of our own actions or the actions of others while here on earth, while afraid, Jesus remained completely "whole" in his "god-consciousness." He was "One with God" and "God with Him" – all through his torturous ordeal.

There are many beautiful analogies to be made when we look at the word "crucifixion" as a form of testing and initiation.

If you stand back, with your eyes spiritually open, or even partially open, you will begin to *see* and *feel* a golden glow of beauty that surrounds the world's suffering.

*(Our Lord wants us to deeply understand
that one cannot appreciate the greatest
glories Heaven provides unless one has
something opposite to compare it to.)*

Suffering offers each soul a chance to break free from its arrogance, its ego, its personality, and its misdirection. Suffering can, depending on the degree of pain, cause one to kneel down, to bend, to become humble, to reach "inward" inside the heart, to reach "upward" towards The Almighty and ask with a depth of feeling perhaps not yet fully felt for heavenly help.

And when the release of such burdens and challenges has passed; when the cause of the suffering is *understood* AND your soul is freed from emotional distress and frustration…always on the other side of suffering (rightly conquered) is **JOY** in equal measure!

You may be deeply "afraid" to be tested.

Try not to be. Trust when I tell you – you are so much stronger than you may believe.

As Bob Marley once said:

> **"You never know how strong you are,
> until being strong is your only choice."**

This is so true of Jesus.

Maybe while reading this you were not aware, but it is a truth that during Jesus' ordeal he was so afraid and in such suffering he "sweated blood." It is a medical condition that does happen when a body is in a type of anguish beyond most people's ability to comprehend – if never experienced.

Think about this. This was Jesus.

Despite the fact that the Lord did not release Jesus from his destiny of arrest and crucifixion, Jesus demonstrated courage and unshakable faith in God as he endured unimaginable torture. He walked carrying his cross while his body bled. He stood under intense injury to his back, legs, and arms. He was held UP and carried by the Lord. He faced his torturers with Godly peace in his eyes and He died on the cross begging our Father in Heaven to "forgive" his accusers.

Jesus faced his destiny with grace, dignity, courage, and forgiveness.

If you step back and reflect on what Jesus, the man, experienced, is there not a touch of "beauty" and (admiration) that you *feel* as you think on how he coped in the face of such unimaginable suffering?

That feeling is loving compassion.

And it is beautiful.

One important secret too as to others in our lives who maybe do not act in order to help "save" us from terrible suffering, it is oftentimes because inaction by others is God's will. And in Jesus' life these persons were Jesus' disciples. Had they acted and spoken up – they too would have been tortured and crucified. If that happened, no one would have survived to tell the stories of Jesus that fill the Holy Bible today. Glorious stories which provide rich nourishment for so many people around the world.

The disciples' hands were "stayed" by God.

And they obeyed.

And what about Judas...do you perceive him as Jesus' enemy? A turncoat – a traitor; well maybe at first glance, but when your spiritual eyes open you will see the beauty and the unconditional love beneath his very special role.

I read once an incredible story by a woman who claimed to be a mystic and who had vivid visions on Jesus, Judas, and his disciples. She saw them before birth in heaven whereby they had agreed with the Lord the earthly roles they would play in Jesus' destiny. They were all "brothers" in heaven and they loved each other unconditionally. The Lord being their "Father" trusted that if he sent them to earth on His mission together, they would each honor their respective roles.

Jesus was Judas' favorite brother in heaven. This woman "saw" that it was Judas who the Lord and Jesus agreed would be the one to *"turn Jesus in."* **Why?** Because Judas understood the importance of **Jesus' purpose** and he loved the Lord and Jesus so completely, so devotedly, that Jesus and the Lord trusted Judas *would not* **NOT** act out his part. He would not fail when the time came. Yet Judas too in his role as a human being *(a man like Jesus)* felt doubt, regret, and fear before he turned Jesus in...but he did as he had promised his Heavenly Father he would do...in order to **"set"** the final act of Jesus' mission on earth in motion.

THAT IS DIVINE LOVE!

And while I have no idea whether there is heavenly "truth" to this story...I love it anyway!

It envelops me in a feeling of such beauty, perfection, trust, and peace that our Creator (who many here on earth visualize as a man sitting on a throne*) is beyond our words to describe GLORIOUS! HE himself is GLORIOUS, HIS "ways" more spectacular in their intention than we can ever hope to understand with our minds. But HE is within us (always) and we can "feel" HIM through our heart (when we ask with sincerity for a direct connection) and in the asking we begin the steps to understand HIM and his way, just as Jesus demonstrated.

A thought – If along your spiritual journey you encounter negative questions designed to challenge or discredit your beliefs...simply smile and know that in some way, this could be a tiny test – it may be God playing a kind of peek-a-boo game with you (I see you but can you see me??).

---

* While it is not my purpose to try and tackle the ageless question of what God looks like, or what form God takes – I do hope to offer...that the mind's need (or our ego's "need") to ask this question...causes an immediate "limitation" to set in, which affects one's ability to "see" past this unanswerable question and may cause blindness to one's *inner sight*. Our human brain simply cannot fathom what form it is that God takes – as God is everywhere and in all things – at all times. I believe he is an indescribable brilliant energy and thought stream which exists **within (all things) yet is (outside all things) AT the exact same time.** Because we are limited in the scope of what our brain can process, we cannot "know" the true answer to this question. But through our hearts we can "feel" our faith and the comfort that it does gift.

Maybe you are being "tested" to see if your faith holds under the inquiry of others. If you can accept that our Creator is everywhere and in "everything" – an illuminating "light of understanding" inside you will "turn on" and be present and within you at all times.

Possibly...then what you may see before you is an alternate "face" of God *teasing you*.

The **"theatre of life"** is God. And as with any game...it is always your choice whether to play or not...

Try to "see and feel" this truth.

It is always **your choice** (while your soul wears its earthly mask) how long you participate in the "theatre of life" God has designed. If you choose and allow yourself to become fully engaged, ENRAGED, entangled, frightened, threatening to others, or even mentally ill – your life will spiral out of control and *off you will go!!*

And for a very long time...

My hope is that as you uncover your "god-consciousness" eyes, they will, once opened, deliver rich spiritual perspective, tremendous compassion, and brotherly understanding resulting in a centered, wholesome, peaceful frame of mind.

You will in time become "immune" to the hysterics of life.

Consider the "theatre of life" as you would a riddle, such as which came first, the chicken or the egg, and move forward on your path without any undue emotional distress.

When you discover spiritual serenity and when you have anchored firmly within your mind and inner body an understanding of what is actually going on in the world (the "theatre of life"), your soul will eventually quit its struggles and the arguments that so often lead to intense personal suffering for you. And from there your growth as a soul will accelerate.

Destiny lies in your hands.

A mystical secret – One of the most exceptional gifts your "god-conscious" eyes deliver is that you will… in steps…transcend judgment (on all things) "human." Divine Forgiveness will birth within, gifting you grace, love, and compassion. These are essential qualities for any soul to feel.

Forgiveness for "your own self" is one of the highest forms of love you can develop. However, there is one more aspect beyond the "holiness" of forgiveness that is even richer and more deeply loving than forgiveness. And that is **Acceptance.**

Forgiveness – in the early stage of one's soul growth – is often extended with a judgmental edge, either unto yourself or onto someone else.

As you embrace Divine Truths and as you ascend towards the Divine Light within, you will transcend forgiveness. You will become ONE with Divine Acceptance.

Acceptance of the ALL that IS

"Acceptance" is an eternal well that combines

together love, divine light, grace, compassion, and forgiveness.

It is the **ALL** that **IS.**

"Acceptance" is Divinity. It is the highest combination of human and spiritual truth we can obtain while here on this earth. And while there are popular spiritual courses, workbooks, and manifestos that teach "forgiveness" as the answer to all things human, I offer that buried deeper within the heart lies a vibrational "hum" called Acceptance that when fully felt offers every soul a resolute strength that is wholly Divine and healing. Embrace it fully...and "see."

Healing Hate

THE CURRENT-DAY REALITY OF HATE-FILLED SPEECH and personal attacks will cease **ONLY** when (in larger and larger numbers) people's counter "reactions" of incredible anger and hate-filled speech in return *stop!*

Divine Laws are absolute in their truth.

What do I mean by that?

Every person's idea...*while they are here on earth...* about what is **"right"** and what is **"true"** is governed by their ego, level of intellect, knowledge of a subject, facts, and acceptance of facts. What might be true in China may not work in the United States.

Cultural thought varies and is relative to the people and nations who live there.

And while the "theatre of life" includes ALL dramas of our humanness, it is essential that you understand that no matter how much you may desire it, you/we cannot change nor should we even think we can try to change **the thoughts or beliefs of others**.

It ALL is "The Game of Life" our Creator has designed.

Your "reaction" to others...you can change!

Your anger, your speech, your retaliation or accusation back onto the other person or persons, even your "fear," starts to engage a *dark energy stream* that if you had eyes to "see" would look like ropes.

You tie yourself to the person you do not agree with (or are afraid of) when your have violent reactions and outbursts. You bind your energy to them in unseen threads of anger and whiplash which can go on and on and on, back and forth...for a very, very long time.

Lifetimes...

With loved ones and family these kinds of energy ties can be devastating.

THINK before you speak. **PRAY** before you react in anger. Begin to understand that your violent *"reaction" jails you, it chains you, and it jails and chains the other person to you.*

This does not mean conscious intellectual disagreements cannot happen. They must happen on this earth for the world to eventually eclipse poverty, ignorance, political challenges, and the wars that recycle.

However, being "awake" and "god-conscious," you will begin to possess an *emotional distancing* and this will gift (you) a kind of *immunity* or protection from unconscious reactionary response.

Your *inner sight* will allow you to "**see**" things from a higher viewpoint.

And you will begin to relax.

Depending on the issue or person you may decide to withdraw your energy from whatever the situation is.

Trust that the correct answer for you – *you will feel and know when you begin to "see" life through the lens of calmness, self-discipline, peace, and love.*

Think on this one message.

If you have come this far in my book, you are sincerely seeking spiritual peace. It may take you, though, many more readings, prayers, and release from relationships or circumstances that no longer serve your higher purpose in life.

Trust!

I believe that our Creator has a wonderful sense of humor and that the ongoing saga of life is pure "theatre."

And (we all) have agreed to be a part of it.

But there is a time when a soul must move on.

And while I have no idea how long this earth reality is to be...I do know that you're suffering from having been in the "game of life" too long...you can begin to transition and come to an end.

You can become free!

If you have recently been angered, felt judged, become afraid of the worldly threats of terrorism, or you have been critically injured, emotionally hurt, or felt humiliated by a loved one, please try my "spiritual cleanse."

It can absolutely help you to dissolve and release any dark energy you may have ingested and been carrying around for a very long time.

Stand under your shower and visualize the water coming down – blend in your mind all the healing colors of the rainbow (red, orange, yellow, green, blue, indigo, and violet). See these colors combining and cleansing your inner body...dissolving and carrying away (down into the drain) your fears, physical pain, feelings of being misunderstood, and your anger.

Ask your inner soul to release all your *ill-ease*.

Perhaps your pain was caused by you trying to make someone else agree with you.

Admit your role in any issue
that needs to be resolved.

Admit as well, when you have done ALL that you can do to bring "healing" into a relationship, a situation, or a friendship...*that it just is not any longer meant to be.*

Honesty is a beautiful thing
when you step into it.

It is a very sacred divine spiritual law that you should not ever take upon yourself the responsibility to "**make**" someone else understand anything.

You cannot force others to grow in their spirituality or to believe what you want for them to believe.

You can only take care of yourself, your thoughts, and your emotions.

Many people walk this earth and will never concern themselves with the feelings or the needs of someone else.

THAT is not your concern.

If you find yourself tied to a cruel, unkind, and toxic human being, you must consider within your heart whether it is time for you to gain release.

Pray to Archangel Michael and ask
for his help to cut the cord.

However KNOW…that if your time with whatever is happening with another person or a complex situation is not (yet) at an end: *you may not be released!*

You must "**earn**" the right to leave problematic situations (through prayer, forgiveness, correct actions, and balanced understanding)…especially if you yourself have been part of the cycle and recycle of pain and suffering.

You must heal yourself and in
time "release" will arrive.

Just saying you are DONE *does not mean you will be.*

You can try to escape, run away, and certainly you should if you feel physical danger for your person…but the **conditions** that set this all in motion may very well come back around to you again and again until the matter or cause is finally fully healed.

Baby steps…

All release and all healings begin the instant you secure within yourself:

Self-control, Understanding, and Acceptance of what has been going on in the saga of life…

Find your way – "The Way" to your heavenly peace waiting within.

The Angels when *asked* can be very helpful.

Begin to stand in the Divine understanding that… *Time is forever*. However, while Universal time IS eternal… healing personal suffering while on earth is measured *in years*.

Nothing within the **"theatre of life"** will repair or heal in one earth day. We will not save our animals, our planet, change our climate, or feed those suffering starvation, homelessness, terrorism, or disease in one month, one year, or even one decade.

No matter – once you accept within yourself (direct connection to your soul) and you gain the benefits, the inner strength and peace that will gift…

You will uncover extraordinary PEACE.

Suddenly, you will feel lighter. Your sleep will be deeper and you will simply agonize less (or not at all) over what others think, feel, or believe. And you will gain an impeccable Trust that the happenings of the world which you personally cannot change...

God in time will heal.

Secure within yourself *Spiritual Perspective*...**and you will live free of all worldly turmoil.**

When you pray, yearn, and desire to transcend what is in truth our collective "human blindness," the light of Divine Love will shine bright...and you will "see" the truth of all things, which once appeared so *dark*.

And you will become calm!

Everything is of God...and it is all GOOD.

How to arrive at this place of *non-judgment*?

While you are here on earth, living, striving, growing towards your own state of "god-consciousness," it is essential to allow inside your soul the Divine Truth and understanding that how you choose to **"react"** to any problem that comes your way will determine how long you either wrestle with or conquer the challenge.

The world churns daily with stories of horror and suffering and oftentimes we must turn our eyes away from it. It can be very disturbing to witness, day after day, the suffering of others we feel powerless to change, but changing yourself and your feeling of helplessness does help in profound magical ways.

You can turn off the TV and say a deep *heart-felt prayer*.

Send light and love to those affected and really, really mean it.

Surround your home, your neighborhood, your family and loved ones with the Divine White Light of Love and Protection. See it in your mind clear and true and wrap yourself and them within it. The more you pray with heartfelt sincerity, deep purpose, and deep trust...you can perform miracles while here on earth.

Reject the inclination to rant and rave (over and over) at the injustice of it all.

Reject as well the inclination to swim in the contaminated waters of fear and ugliness, as can happen when you absorb too much of what can be seen on TV and social media outlets. The current-day news on the horrific acts being committed in different parts of the world must be offset by light workers' acts of love, prayer, and calmness. It is time to begin (all of us) with conscious intent to view some of the horrors happening as we would any scary movie. Do not allow the energy vibration of fear to destroy your peace of mind or your faith in God. Choose to not watch, not absorb, stay centered, calm, trusting, and pray...offer prayers of white light and love and you will be one of God's light workers!

Begin to send strong intentional light, love, and peace to those who need it most while they battle (for whatever reason) the darkness that has descended upon them. No matter that; hold your spiritual perspective...

There is GOOD everywhere in

**the world, even in those places
where it appears hopeless.**

Stories are all around us of heroes who save others from terrible fates.

We see on the Internet wonderful rescue stories of animals neglected, abused, and thrown away. But almost always these animals forgive and love again – if given the chance.

We watch stories of strangers risking their lives to save others from flood waters, fires, and earthquakes.

There is divine, courageous love everywhere.

How many times have you marveled and had your heart melt over images as we can find daily on the Internet on divine acts of love and compassion in motion? It may be children with disabilities who do incredible things with their bodies never thought possible. Wounded Warriors, who walk again, smile again, love again. Today there are thousands of people who have been witnesses to or victims of demonic acts of terrorism who have escaped, lived, and have healed. They smile again, pick up their lives, and hold trust in God with all their hearts.

Heroic acts of courage can be
found everywhere on earth.

**Goodness is defeating
negativity all around us.**

Allow you inner soul to "see" and "know" it for what it is. It is God's love being acted out in counter-balance to life's negative events. And once you do see it, embrace this divine love fully inside your own heart.

It will help you while you walk your own path.

Good counters Bad – Love counters Hate.

Once you begin to gain inner strength and if you consciously accept as a new purpose being one of God's Light Workers while here on earth, oftentimes, we may still find ourselves facing over and over the exact same difficulty, which has long troubled us. It may arrive back around repackaged in other people, events, and issues…

**The soul's goal while here on earth is
to transcend that which it must learn.**

Individual choice, free will really, is God's greatest gift to us all.

We can choose to remain **asleep, numb, and indifferent** to what is occurring to us or we can *"awaken."*

**We can choose joy and compassion,
patience and love!**

Or we can relapse back into pain and suffering.

No angelic being or guardian angel can intercede and take away from you the difficulties you may face while here on earth.

*And you do not want them to be
taken away from you.*

Choose to face each difficulty **with dignity, trust, grace, and strength**.

Hopefully with the inner knowledge that such circumstances have appeared for your greatest good.

It is in the facing of each of life's problems, with confidence and without fear, THAT the ultimate form of initiation occurs.

Whether you are Christian, Buddhist, Muslim, Hindu, or Jewish, try to visualize the lessons and the teachings of those who came before us. Abraham, Moses, Jesus, Mohammad, and Buddha each faced unique lessons while here on earth designed for universal learning and benefit.

**The highest of these is that
we are all LOVED.**

So wherever you are, *know that all is well – always*.

If you are in your later years, grieving those *things you wish you never did, never said, never thought...*

Forgive yourself.

Forgive, forgive, forgive, and allow your soul to surrender. You can and will do better next time.

There will always be a next time – **that is what the greatest secret of all is.**

We come back. We get to try again. And in that rebirth...how we choose to meet our tests must be with less worry, anxiety, hatred and pain.

Our Tomorrow is created today.

Karma – Balance

KARMA'S ROLE IN OUR LIVES IS SO OFTEN MISUNDERstood by us. It has been mangled about in many distorted ways. However, it is important to understand that at the core of the Creator's love is everything, all life, human, energetic, all – is striving towards **Balance**. The scales of the universe demand that light/dark, yin/yang, good/bad are in exact equal measure.

This is a most difficult truth for most souls to learn, accept, and surrender to. Many religions preach "you reap what you sow," and very often it is interpreted in terms of judgment, harshness, vengeance, and pity.

This has never been true.

God punishes no one!!

All of your personal experiences are happening because you "thought" or "brought" them into reality either in this lifetime or a previous one. There are many books to read on this Divine Truth alone. But know this.

The entire Universe is one big huge scale.

At the most microscopic level of all – *life lies in perfect balance.*

And your higher self is working every moment of your life to align **balance** within you, so your life can be one that transcends its lessons.

Karma is one of the ways to describe this process.

However, Karma alone is not enough.

Learn to live your life awakened and aware that all experiences that come to you and those you love, all trials, suffering and even times of joy are happening in concert to guide your soul, your spirit – towards total perfect balance.

Each time you see the benefits of what comes about will enable you to "accept" and "welcome" with less struggle those difficult trials and tests that will come.

Your attitude and feelings about what seems annoying and disturbing can be realigned.

No one can live a life that is ALL JOY – No pain, ALL PAIN – no joy.

Accept your trials with a grateful and thankful heart, without the need to bemoan it as being unfair.

Nothing in life really is unfair.

It just IS – what is – (because) – what is – needs to be – for your soul's growth to wholeness and peace.

When you go about handling each disappointment with dignity, honesty, and calmness – *catching the flow* of all that the universe offers…you will finally be on the other side.

As long as you remain here on this earth, your soul will be striving to help you achieve perfect balance in order for you to transcend the need for coming back here again.

Capturing this very special **Knowing** is the key to incredible emotional peace!

For myself, before I allowed this knowing inside my soul and heart, when I was busy in my life and career – I was always distracted.

When home, I was worried about my customers.

When I was visiting my customers, I was worried about my home, my animals, and my employees.

When I was out straight working – I was thinking on how I needed a vacation.

When on vacation – I was thinking about the office.

Crazy disjointed and distracted thoughts whip-lashed me all the time. I began to misinterpret **"why"** certain circumstances were happening. Tight cash flow resulted in my losing sleep until it resolved. A huge new customer and their first order would mean I would attend to every single detail of that new order's process like a mother hen. I was on top of everything! I did not give myself or my employees (who were doing a great job) a break. Check, double-check, re-check…it never ended. If I walked into the office one day and saw the wall calendar on the wrong month, I would have a meltdown! I would immediately think, "if this calendar is on the wrong month...what else is happening that I cannot see?"

I was obsessed with every little thing, painfully so. While my staff loved me, I made them nervous.

I made myself nervous, but I ran a great operation and there were few to no unexpected disappointments.

However, this kind of grind and stress wore me down emotionally, physically, and mentally. What I thought to be Karma (or my destiny) was in fact a misunderstanding of several spiritual principles. I felt I had to "MAKE" my company's reality...real. I had to "FORCE" results – rather than allow results to just appear due to good decisions.

I exhausted myself.

When I met my husband I began a new life, which meant a lot more relaxation and time off. And despite my not being on top of every single detail – my company ran fantastically.

The basics, the momentum, and all of the operating procedures were in place. I no longer needed to babysit every minute, of every day, for the results to remain as we had become accustomed to.

My life gained a little bit of that **BALANCE** so important for true spiritual growth.

Once I achieved that, I erroneously believed I was at the peak of my life. I wasn't.

I was enjoying a form of recreation that every soul deserves, but I still had lessons to face and pass.

I "called" these lessons to me.

And while I understood much and I was a very kind person – I was still yet "untested."

Then my leukemia arrived.

That was KARMA'S attempt to "test" and bring wholeness to my soul. My leukemia was a spiritual testing that I was ready for.

I did not *knowingly* ask for this test, I did not *will* it to happen; it just did because a bell – just like in school – went off.

And ready or not…my soul faced later on another great testing – the closure of my business.

That test aligned my soul finally with the Balance my higher self was truly seeking.

And while to outsiders it may seem cruel that my leukemia appeared when I was feeling on top of the world… that is just not the case. I was "ready" to be tested.

One way to make sense of these universal "testings" – Karma, initiation, etc. – is to think, does a loving competent school teacher not "test" her students, in order for them to graduate? Now, if she has properly prepared them and they have themselves been good students and have not cheated a bit here and there, well…a passing grade will result!

**Tomorrows are being built
every second of every day.**

If you want to be fortified, solid, faith filled, and confident, you must begin to live each day as *kind*, as awake, *and as loving as you can.*

A major test or initiation for you may not occur during this lifetime, but it may happen to someone you love.

And again how you react, how you handle such terrible difficulty, is a "testing" for your soul too.

If my words are reaching you now deep inside your heart, know that when you meet each of life's tests with an unshakable faith – even if you have struggled during your life with thoughts that you have not ever been "good enough" (maybe not so kind, so loving) – in one second of insight – *heart-felt prayer, understanding, and forgiveness – **you will be transformed.***

One of the greatest gifts I hope you will take from my book is this: When you are ready, really (really) ready to transcend the suffering you have been experiencing and when you allow one, two, or more of the divine truths inside your heart...

**Your soul will hear that "click"...
that connection to ALL that is.**

No matter if it does not happen right away for you, Trust. Know that when your soul is ready...really ready...IT will happen in an instant.

It took me years to understand *one more very special sacred deep truth.*

**And that truth is that what appears
as negativity in life is of God.**

All things which appear Terrible are of God and

all things which we do not fully understand are God. All of it!

Our Creator has his ways….many of which we will never fully understand while here on earth.

Releasing your need to be in full control ("opinion-ated") as to all things, every event, every tragedy, and every minute of every day…will bless your life with an ease, a FLOW, *a richness of "quiet" that will aid you in unimaginable ways.*

Balance – you will gain a sense of equilibrium that will allow you to "see" the purpose of what may be occurring so that you can join "god-consciously" in the positive outcome for yourself, all those involved, our world, blessing from the heart – your heart the highest good for all people!

Your heart will act as your compass.

**Trust then in the Wisdom of your own
Heart – it will guide you safely home.**

CHAPTER NINE

Divine Peace at Long Last

N THIS WORLD THERE ARE HUNDREDS OF SPIRITUAL BOOKS for you to read, all there to aid in your personal journey. I recommend that you read as many as you need to come round full circle, back to yourself as our Creator intended, so that your soul's journey for peace can at long last be yours.

While reading is wonderful, your spiritual reading and even the benefits of your community church will fly out the window – *until you learn to accept certain truths about our Creator, his purpose for us in this life, and our personal responsibility to achieve wholeness through acceptance, understanding, and alignment with Divine Love.*

Many of you reading my words may want badly to make the leap into **Trust** and **Acceptance** of God's ways, but in the back of your mind you are still processing some "insult" or "injury" that happened to you during your life.

You cannot let go!

Maybe for you it is about "abandonment." Maybe someone or many people in your life that you loved suddenly left you. Alone, dejected and confused, you blamed God.

"WHY???" WHY did this happen – you just cannot get past...***it.***

Despite the many spiritual works, meditation classes, yoga, church group meetings, or sermons, you are still outraged!!

Whatever is the cause...maybe you were emotionally cheated, stolen from, violated physically, mentally, or maybe you witnessed terrible abuse to someone else or upon yourself, maybe a parent or a loved one humiliated you.

You refuse to let go and be healed.

While you read my words, or the words of others, you try hard to "get it," but you cannot stop shaking your fist in the air while screaming as loudly as you can – "it was...**UNFAIR**"!

"I was treated so unfairly!!!!!"

Rest in the knowledge that this outrage cannot lift away from you until you are done learning whatever lessons being so thoroughly mistreated are meant to teach you.

TRUST...

Everything that happens to you is delivered unto you because it brings with it a spiritual gift.

Especially those events which appear most terrible...

they often arrive because your soul is ready for these things to happen in order for you to grow.

Maybe in a past life you did not face the challenge.

Maybe you somehow *"skated"* and did not take the spiritual karmic test seriously at all.

Facing it steadfastly until it was concluded...

The Universe is a master record-keeper.

IT KNOWS ALL.

A very special Universal Truth.

Your higher self and your guardian angel **KNOW** everything you have ever done, every thought you think, and all your deeds.

I personally feel that part of the grander purpose for the current-day issue of "privacy" is to enlighten all people to the reality...that there is never (anywhere) true privacy!

**Nothing in the Universe
under God is secret.**

You cannot commit any crime and not have a stain upon your soul that someday you will need to **BAL-ANCE** right with a counter-action.

This is one of the greatest spiritual truths.

Meeting your life's tests with calmness, certainty of purpose, dignity, and acceptance will speed you on your way back **HOME**.

It is said that the gates to Heaven will not open until your soul "rings" a certain note.

**That *"note"* is unconditional
PEACE and LOVE.**

When it lives inside your heart, the kingdom of heaven opens. It cannot help but open – it is God's greatest promise to us all.

Trust that no matter however long you take, no matter how many lifetimes it may be, you are within your soul right now… striving to find your way HOME.

We all are. And we will ALL get there.

**Life is Eternal, Time has no Meaning, God
is Pure Love, and the Universe = Balance.**

Every action and **reaction** in your life determines how long your journey as a soul will last.

"A thousand years is but one day in heaven," it is written. Imagine how many lifetimes and chances we are given.

Is God not wonderful!

We will all find our way home, no matter who, no matter where. No matter that bombs still destroy towns and villages here on earth. No matter the ongoing confusing conflict amongst different religions and countries…

**WE ARE ALL PART of the pattern of the
Universe. ALL of us are a part of GOD.**

So take your time and take a deep breath. There is no rush when you view life in the big picture of time. Really embrace this and watch your soul relax.

You will begin to walk a bit slower in your life – there really is no use rushing.

Speed will not get you there faster.

The **FLOW** of the divine will aid you in every step. Watch your body relax as minor irritations and confusion arise. No need to **REACT** as if your world is coming apart. It is not.

Greet each situation like an old friend.

Say *"Ah…so you're here again, are you?"*…whatever the difficulty may be. Each time you welcome and accept difficult events that come to your life – without struggle – you will have an innate power to dissolve whatever it is…almost without effort.

This is one of God's promised gifts to each soul.

The better acquainted with this that you get, the easier it becomes and fewer struggles result.

If for any reason a major catastrophe happens, know that this event is an important "testing" for you to trust in.

If in your past you avoided minor, small testings, understand that the Universe recycles this lesson meant for you – **next time packaged a little more intensely.**

Your problems or obstacles will become larger and more difficult until you have resolved each properly…

Resent nothing, no one, and no event. It is all arriving for your highest and greatest good.

Walk with peace, kindness, loving gentleness, steadfast courage, and self-control, and watch your life become amazing in every respect.

TODAY CREATES TOMORROW – And tomorrow leads you safely HOME.

May love and light be yours forever.

Words to Hold Close
to Your Heart

Prayers and meditative thoughts
*from White Eagle's Teachings**

Learning to use your inner senses:

God our Father, in whom we live and move and have our being, we would become aware of Thy love and wisdom. We would open our eyes that we may walk forward into the light, and our ears that we may hear the voice of the spirit, and be channels for the power and radiance of Thy Truth. May Thy light dispel the darkness of earth, and may Thy love bring peace into the hearts of men. May the spirit of peace,

---

*   Excerpts taken from White Eagle's books – Spiritual Unfoldment (books 2 & 3) – White Eagle Publishing Trust.

*and tranquility and calm reign supreme in our
hearts forever. Amen*

The Power of Alchemy – changing dense earthly existence in spiritual freedom and beauty:

*We raise our consciousness to the Most High,
to the Infinite Spirit, our Father-Mother God.
May we be strengthened in the light of His Son,
Christ, the perfect man of earth and heaven....
May his beauty inspire our lives and work; His
wisdom direct our lives and work; and his Love
make manifest His work in us, through us, in all
living things. Amen*

*Follow the One, avoid the many, be true to your
inner light, and the mysteries of the invisible
worlds will be revealed to the degree that you are
ready and will use the knowledge thus attained
in selfless service.*

*Endeavor as you look on any physical form to
see into that form and to the spirit. See it in the
very roots of the trees, in the trunk, branches and
the leaves. Look always for the spirit behind or
within all form*

Never fear Evil while here on Earth:

*The question arises in your mind, Can the
angels of darkness, these angelic forces perhaps
not yet fully aware of the light and the power
and the wisdom of the Most High, triumph over
the angels of light and thus cause the destruction*

of humanity? The answer is **no**! *The dark angels can go only so far and no further because then they are caught up in a cosmic law which renders them powerless.* **God does not allow the universe to slip out of His hands.** *Nothing can happen outside the will of God.*

Your Thoughts have Power: Angels

We endeavor to help you to increase your awareness of angel beings. Some are assisting you to become more conscious of the glorious powers with which God has endowed you, and to become conscious of the power of God Himself. Others are working, building with the material which you offer them through your thoughts and aspirations.

We want you to realize that your thoughts are drawn by magnetic attraction towards other thought streams either positive or negative. All positive thoughts – by this we mean uplifting, constructive thoughts – by the law of attraction join great streams of thought which are good, which are of the White Light. Negative, unkind or cruel thoughts are in their turn used to swell the great streams of darkness. Oh, how much unconscious cruelty there is! Thoughtlessness can cause much suffering, and is therefore a form of cruelty. On the other hand, your thoughtfulness and kindness, whatever form it takes, is a contribution to that great stream of White Light upon which humanity is depending for its very existence. You can contribute to it by your thoughts;

and all that you withhold is robbing humanity of the life – of air if you like.

What a responsibility rests on those who know this truth! Think of these things and resolutely determine to give love and light to the great ocean of life. Resolve here and now that you will never fail to give the right thought, the right emotion, the right feeling to life and all your brethren.

Further:

Is not life grand and rich? Is it not worth every effort to gain mastery, and use your God-given powers? Never think that you are alone or that you can live to yourself, for only yourself, for all around you are Great Ones, not only human but also of the angelic kingdom.

Guardian Angels:

For each one of you has not only a human companion or guide in spirit, but also a **guardian angel** who comes from heavenly states of life, from supernal states and has you in his/her care. Many, many times does your guardian angel draw close, but it is only in its tranquil moments that the soul is receptive to the ministry of angels. Often you are so concerned with the world and with yourself that you are deaf to the promptings of your guardian angel.

May your imagination reveal to you the glorious form of your own guardian angel, that *messenger sent by God to help you through all the experiences of your life on earth.*

Words to calm the mind's need to intellectualize the glories of Heaven:

Eye hath not seen, nor ear heard...the things which God hath prepared for them that love him.

Your limited consciousness cannot comprehend these glories; nor can you realize the vast unseen life which is all around you. But meditation (quietness) will help you towards this inner vision and realization. Remember those elder brethren (angels) who traversed the same path as every soul must tread. They understand, and they come to help you on the path which leads to spiritual realization and illuminations, and union with God.

Death:

The Angel of Death is not a gruesome spectre as imagined, nor cold or cruel. Draw aside the veil of the Angel of Death, and you will see a face of ineffable mercy, compassion and love revealed. We would like you to understand that all life is held in God's love and preparation is made for all the important events in man's life. We would have you think of the Great White Spirit as One Who ever loves you. Remember children, that God, your Father-Mother-God, will never, never, forsake you. Jesus said, "Even the very hairs on your head are numbered," and "not a sparrow falls to the ground without your Father in heaven…"

You are held closely in His love and in the care of His ministering angels. Ask, seek, and you will receive in full measure blessings both spiritual and physical, for this is Divine Law in operation. Divine Law never fails.

From My Heart to Yours

HAVE WRITTEN THIS INSPIRATIONAL BOOK IN THE HOPES you will find it to be an indispensable guide on your spiritual journey of understanding our incredible universe. While I know that it is never possible to understand *everything* that happens in life and the *"whys"* of it all, I do know it is possible to understand much of it.

No matter how many spiritual or mystical books you have read, it is a **divine truth** that until you are *finally ready to be released from pain and suffering,* **you will not be.**

But, you can begin in "one moment" to make a great change and my deepest desire is that my words within will help.

Ever since I was a young girl, I have had OBEs – out-of-body experiences. I astral projected when I was very young and during my college years I used to fall into a "swoon" whereby vivid visions would play out in front of my eyes like a movie theater screen. When I was 42 years old I had a near-death experience.

I wrote about a few of these experiences in my memoir, *A Soft Landing*. This book details not only my personal life's struggles and suffering, but my spiritual journeys to find the answers so many are searching for.

People often question whether it is possible for them to really, (really) know what it feels like to be "free" from the body and to taste the indescribable peace and glory, being so near death or (the doorway to the afterlife) "gifts" and the honest answer is – *I am not sure*. When I meditate or pray, no matter how long, intense, or amazing the feelings I experience, it cannot compare in the exact way as what I (and many others) have experienced as I stood before the doorway to the "afterlife."

Words simply fail to convey the depth of "feeling" the utter timeless of it all, the peace, comfort, and completeness. It is a feeling of wholeness that is indescribable – although I try hard to offer as much of it as I can.

I do know that it is not necessary to have an NDE (near-death experience) to gain immense benefit from your accepting some or all of the Divine Truths I have shared within this book.

I believe spontaneous profound "knowing" can occur when sacred words are interwoven together whereby a kind of artful beauty is *felt*...and which can then trigger inner "sight" to become tantalized and opened. I have attempted to weave and interlace for you (in steps) both aspects of what my life in pain and suffering was like...and what my life is like now as I live in peace…so that you…(in baby steps) draw within you an essence of the "hum" that lives inside me.

Discovering your divinity and sacredness as a soul is the most liberating and "freeing" act you can do for yourself. Money cannot buy and there is nowhere on this earth you can travel to, whereby you will uncover mysteries more incredible than the magic that lives right inside you now, in this moment and forever. Discovery and exploration into one or all of the Divine Truths I write about will crack this doorway (inside you) to open. And within every Divine Truth there are layers and layers of deeper spiritual truths and sacred secrets that you can uncover and discover for yourself… as your own spiritual eyes and your heart open. Loneliness, fear, and misunderstandings will slowly ebb away.

There are no romance novels, adventure stories, or mystery writings that can compare to the incredible excitement you will feel when you begin to fully understand how incredible you really are as a soul here on earth! Nothing is as magnificent as this self-discovery. All the things you may have needed to help you to cope with your past or hardships will vanish *eventually*. It can begin in small baby steps, one divine truth at a time.

It is a joyous adventure…and it is all yours.

– I love spiritual symbolism –

It is a truth that Spiritual Wisdom is best understood in simple terms. Every Divine Truth contains within it…*an indescribable elegance and rich beauty.*

I have come to learn for myself that there is really

no lasting benefit to be found in some of the intensely complicated approaches a few spiritual teachers have prescribed. "Tomes" do not need to be read in order for you to gain spiritual insight and peace. However, they can be rollicking great reads and a lot of fun to talk about with others. You will absolutely gain some benefit.

It is not until you *reach inward* and claim *connection to your soul* – that a lasting concrete change inside yourself can be built.

For you to be truly ready to survive life's toughest testings, you must be fortified deep inside your heart and soul.

In writing about divine truths, I found that there was an inherent complex challenge in how best to lay out this information...as every reader is uniquely on his/her own spiritual journey. There really was no academic way to bullet-point the divine truths and say this is the only way for your soul to learn and grow. Such a method creates a feeling of constriction and can feel dogmatic...and is why so many people reject religion and/or religious teachings. Your individual soul may disallow being asked to learn or understand any particular divine truth, in one order or another, because each one of us is on this earth at an entirely different place, on our road Home to God.

And the good news is – you do not need to accept any one of them in any specific order.

This alone is one the most important spiritual truths there is.

**Every soul is unique and individual.
There is no one way!**

You yourself may be very hungry and eager in your search for spiritual learning and the comfort that it gifts – and yet your spouse may appear to be sound asleep. Does that make your spouse bad or negligent? Absolutely not! He/she may be far more advanced inside his/her own soul in terms of its learning...than you could possibly know.

They may just be napping!

Life, while often so wonderful...can be fraught with constant distractions, general malaise, loneliness, frustration, illness, complex financial tragedies, and unexpected global events.

You may go years without feeling the need to nourish your soul in any spiritual way. But then something will occur to you or someone you love and BAM, like that...you're flattened and in intense emotional, mental, and/or physical suffering. It will be during times like these that hopefully a book like this could be what your soul most needs in order to find inner peace.

*– A little bit of that spiritual
symbolism for you –*

I think **The Wizard of Oz** is one of the most amazing spiritual stories every told. And the words God, our Lord, or Universe are never spoken. Not once. But it is a most spectacular story about the sacred beauty of how our Universe and Lord Creator works.

Let me share here a bit of what I mean.

The tornado (a symbol of spiritual testing) sweeps Dorothy and her little dog up into "it" and off they go. They land in a strange world and have colorful scary adventures, meeting new friends, and together they experience exotic realities. Dorothy meets a good white angel and an evil dark one too!

*At every turn Dorothy is surprised by the things she discovers. She meets all kinds of new "beings" and Dorothy is led to search for (**a man**) whom she is given to believe is the only "**ONE**" who can help her find her way Home…(a warning not to allow false prophets or glamorizing gurus into your life). When at last Dorothy is tired and lonely for **HOME**, despite the fact she has all these new friends in her life, the depth of her inner longing – **to GO HOME – brings the answer**. (This is a symbolic reference to the soul's yearning to find its way home – our Heavenly Home of safety, peace and unconditional love.)*

And HOME is available to us all
while we are here on earth.

*With the help of the good white witch…Dorothy discovers all along that she had (within) her **The Way HOME**.*

It had been in her possession the entire time!

*Dorothy's **red shoes** (red being the color of the **Heart** and **personal power**, symbolized by the bright ruby red)*

TRUE LOVE – DIVINE LOVE

No matter your life's experiences or adventures – the

good, the scary, the false prophets and maybe even some misdirection – like Dorothy you can find your way home. It is my deepest hope that my book can be for you *a yellow brick road…to help guide you on your journey.*

"There is no place like HOME" – "There is no place like HOME."

In love and light. Stacey.

Recommended Reading

(in no specific order)

1. *Illuminata* – Marianne Williamson

2. *Secrets of the Lost Mode of Prayer* – Gregg Braden

3. *Conversations with God* – Neale Donald Walsch

4. *Many Lives, Many Masters* – Dr. Brian Weiss

5. *Only Love is Real* – Dr. Brian Weiss

6. *I Can See Clearly Now* – Dr. Wayne W. Dyer

7. *Everyday Grace* – Marianne Williamson

8. All writings and teachings of White Eagle

9. *E-Squared: Energy Experiments That Prove Your Thoughts Create Reality* – Pam Grout

10. *The Divine Matrix* – Gregg Braden

Reading Group Discussion Questions

1. Have you ever had a NDE (near-death experience) or known someone who has?

2. How did this change your view of religion, heaven, or God?

3. Which Divine Truth is most compelling or special to you and why?

4. Does the author's belief in Divine Truths help you in the understanding of the soul's journey while here on earth?

5. Do you believe Angels exist? Can you hear yours? Do you believe Angels can leave "signs"?

6. Do you believe God is Pure Love?

7. What is the most important part of the book for you??

8. Do you believe we come back to earth again?

9. Do you believe that our thoughts create our reality?

10. If you could ask the author one question – what would that question be?

If you wish to contact the author you may visit her website at http://staceyblake.com; or email here directly at – asoftlanding@staceyblake.com